How Artists See CITIES

Streets Buildings Shops Transportation

Colleen Carroll

ABBEVILLE KIDS

A DIVISION OF ABBEVILLE PUBLISHING GROUP

New York London

"Painters understand nature and love her and teach us to see her."

—VINCENT VAN GOGH

To Avice, with love and thanks.

I'd like to thank the many people who helped make this book happen, especially my editor, Jackie Decter; Ed Decter; Colleen Mohyde; Patricia Fabricant; Jennifer O'Connor; Scott Hall; Jo-Anne Faruolo; and, as always, my husband, Mitch Semel.

—COLLEEN CARROLL

JACKET AND COVER FRONT: Gustave Caillebotte, *Paris Street; Rainy Day,* 1876–77 (see also pp. 4–5). JACKET AND COVER BACK, LEFT: Vladimir Tatlin, *Monument to the Third International,* 1919. © Estate of Vladimir Tatlin/Licensed by VAGA New York, NY (see also pp. 16–17); RIGHT: André Derain, *Charing Cross Bridge,* c. 1906. © 1998 Artists Rights Society (ARS), New York/ADAGP, Paris (see also p. 33). JACKET BACK, BOTTOM: Richard Estes, *Central Savings,* 1975 (see also pp. 24–25).

EDITOR: Jacqueline Decter
DESIGNER: Jennifer O'Connor
PRODUCTION EDITOR: Meredith Wolf Schizer
PRODUCTION MANAGER: Lou Bilka

ISBN-13: 978-0-7892-0187-4
ISBN-10: 0-7892-0187-9

First library edition
10 9 8 7 6 5 4

Library of Congress Cataloging-in-Publication Data
Carroll, Colleen.
Cities : streets, buildings, shops, transportation / Colleen Carroll.
p. cm. — (How artists see,
ISSN 1083-821X)
Includes bibliographical references (p.).
Summary: Examines how cities have been depicted in works of art from different time periods and places.
ISBN 0-7892-0187-9
1. Cities and towns in art—Juvenile literature. 2. Visual perception—Juvenile literature. [1. Cities and towns in art. 2. Art appreciation.] I. Title. II. Series: Carroll, Colleen. How artists see.
N8217.C35C27 1999
704.9'44—dc21 98-46583

For bulk and premium sales and for text adoption procedures, write to Customer Service Manager, Abbeville Press, 137 Varick Street, New York, NY 10013, or call 1-800-ARTBOOK.

CONTENTS

STREETS

PARIS STREET; RAINY DAY

Gustave Caillebotte

What comes to mind when you think of bright lights, busy people, tall buildings, and more sounds than you can imagine? Cities, of course! Cities are some of the world's most exciting places. Maybe that is why so many artists live and work in cities, and try to capture their unique qualities.

As you read this book, you will discover how some artists see four aspects of every city: streets, buildings, shops, and transportation. If you live in a city, the pictures may look very familiar to you, and if you don't, you will begin to discover the energy and excitement of city life—as artists do.

Take a trip back in time to the 1870s, and stroll down this busy street in Paris, France. The picture looks so real, it's easy to imagine yourself doing just that. To create this realistic quality, the painter made the picture very big—so big that the people in the foreground are actually life-size (the painting is nearly seven feet tall). The couple on the right glance across the picture at something you can't see. What do you think they are looking at?

STREETS

EARLY SUNDAY MORNING

Edward Hopper

Cities aren't always noisy, as you can see in this picture of a city street on a bright Sunday morning. There isn't a person in sight. Where could everyone be? Imagine walking down this street all by yourself. What do you think it would feel like? The red, white, and blue barber's pole stands like a piece of peppermint candy in front of the barbershop. There are other shops, too. What types of businesses might they be?

Even though there aren't any people in the picture, the artist makes the street come to life with bold blocks of color. How many colors do you see? The morning sun bathes the scene in light, and creates dark shadows on the buildings and street. Point to all the places where you see shadows.

THE JOCKEY CLUB

Archibald Motley

Unlike the street in the picture you just saw, this street is hopping with energy. Elegantly dressed people step out for an evening on the town at one of the city's nightclubs. Couples stroll arm in arm, a policeman keeps watch on his beat, and a woman walks her little dog on a leash. What words come to mind when you look at this picture?

Even though it is evening, the street is aglow with light, which gives the picture a feeling of romance and drama. Yellow light pours from the street lamp and the car's headlights. In what other places can you find sources of light? Which light seems the brightest to you?

JOCKEY

名所江戸百景
広重画

STREETS

MOONLIT STREET SCENE IN EDO

Hiroshige

Today the Japanese city of Tokyo is home to millions of people. Here you see what a Tokyo street looked like about 150 years ago. This long street is crowded with merchants and passersby going about their business. Starting at the bottom of the picture, walk down the street with your eyes until you reach the end. You've probably noticed that the rows of buildings on the sides of the street form two diagonal lines that seem to meet in the distance. At this point, where do your eyes want to take you next?

The full moon illuminates all the people in the street. What other sources of light do you see? If this picture were a postcard you were sending to a friend, how would you describe this city street?

THE MEETING (MARCHESE LUDOVICO GONZAGA MEETING SON, CARDINAL FRANCESCO G.)

Andrea Mantegna

There's a saying that goes, "On a clear day you can see forever." In this panorama of a hilltop city in Italy, you can almost do just that. The artist gives you an unlimited view of the walled city—from the valley below all the way to the summit. Although the city is seen from a distance, you can see many interesting details, such as Roman ruins and the stonework of the city's walls. What other unusual details can you find? The building at the very top of the hill is the largest of them all. It must be very important to have such a position. Who do you think lives or works there?

If you look carefully, you will see people busily going in and out of the city. What types of jobs are they doing? The serious-looking men in the foreground stand as stiffly as the statue on the hill. Who do you think they are?

CHAGALL

PARIS THROUGH THE WINDOW

Marc Chagall

In this picture of Paris the artist places you in a room to give you a clear view out the window. As you look, you will notice many buildings in the distance, especially the Eiffel Tower. The artist used lots of simple shapes to create all these buildings. How many different shapes can you find?

Some artists change how things really look to give you a certain feeling or to help you see something in a new way. This strange cityscape seems to come from a dream. The artist used color in unusual ways, such as the blue-faced man, the bright yellow cat, and the multicolored sky. What other things do you see that surprise you?

MONUMENT TO THE THIRD INTERNATIONAL

Vladimir Tatlin

Is it a birdhouse? Is it a roller coaster? Just what exactly is it? It's a building! Well, not an actual building, but an architectural model of one. Chances are you've never seen a building quite like this before. The artist who designed this model was trying to create a tower unlike any other. If it had been built, it would have stood 1,300 feet high!

This artist believed that art should be composed of simple shapes and forms. Inside the tower are four forms that seem to float in space, such as the half sphere near the top. There are three others. Can you name them? Surrounding the forms is an elegant spiral frame. Imagine yourself winding your way up the ramp until you reach the top. How's the view from up there? What do you see?

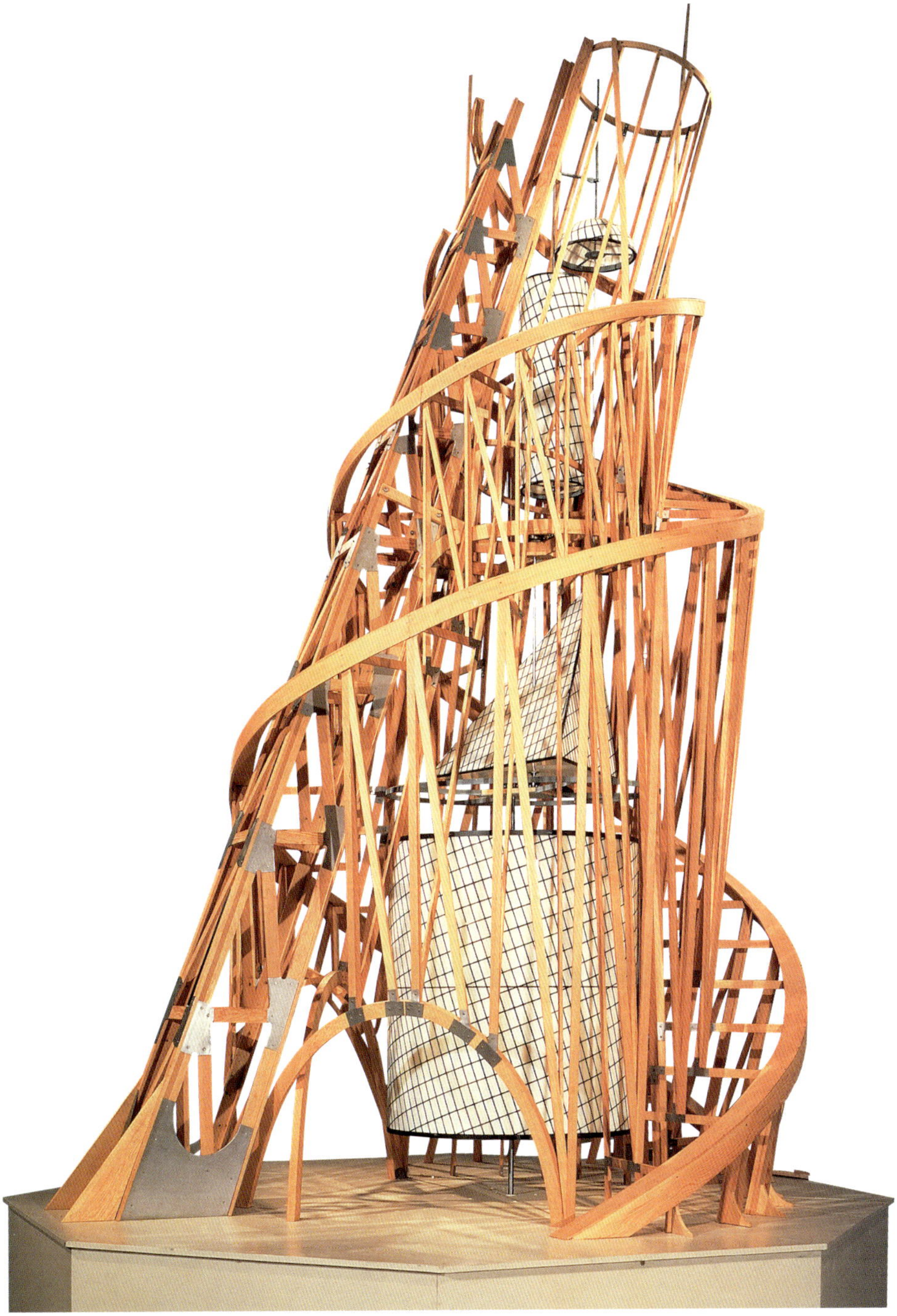

RADIATOR BUILDING, NIGHT, NEW YORK

Georgia O'Keeffe

What would a modern city be without its buildings—its museums, its apartment houses, and of course, its skyscrapers? The artists who made the paintings on these two pages were inspired by the high-rise buildings of New York City—glittering towers of light, steel, glass, and concrete. In the picture on this page it's easy to recognize the building shining brightly against the night sky. Trace your finger around its rectangular shape. What other rectangles can you find?

BROADWAY BOOGIE-WOOGIE

Piet Mondrian

This artist, too, was fascinated by the skyscrapers of New York City. But instead of making a picture of actual buildings, he tried to capture the pattern of horizontal and

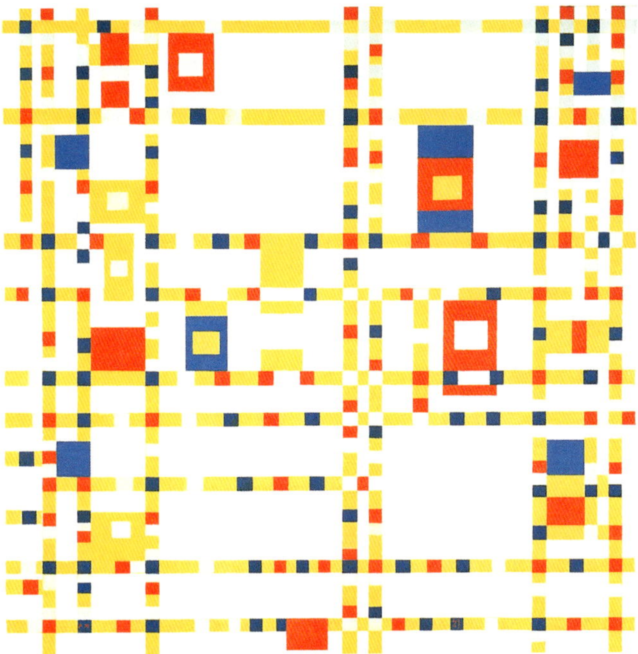

vertical lines that form the city's streets and the effect of the thousands of windows that light up at night. To experience what the artist felt as buildings lit up across the city, blink your eyes quickly while staring at the picture. Which colors "twinkle" the most? The artist named his painting after a popular style of music with strong beats that repeat over and over again. How do the bright colors and simple shapes create this boogie-woogie rhythm?

SPRING SALE AT BENDEL'S

Florine Stettheimer

What city would be complete without its fabulous shops: boutiques, markets, cafes, bodegas, delicatessens, and department stores, to name just a few? A famous New York City store is the scene of this shopping frenzy. The artist gives you a peek inside as women browse through, select, and try on the store's selection of fashions. The painting's vivid colors capture the chaos and energy of the shoppers. Which colors seem to "jump" off the canvas the most? Imagine this same picture in black and white. How would the mood change?

If you didn't know this was a department store, you might think it was a scene in a play, complete with red velvet curtains opened to reveal the actors, costumes, and sets. In fact, most of the shoppers move as if they were dancing: bending, stretching, and twisting their bodies this way and that. Why do you think the artist chose to show these people in such dramatic positions?

MAGASIN, AVENUE DES GOBELINS (SHOP WINDOW, TAILOR DUMMIES)

Jean-Eugène-Auguste Atget

Want to go window shopping? In this photograph of a tailor shop window, four handsomely dressed mannequins display the spiffy fashions of the day. But that's not all. Look carefully and you'll notice things in the window

that aren't for sale. Because the artist took the photo from outside, you can see the reflection of the street off the glass window. Look at the dummy in the middle of the picture and the tree that seems to grow up through his body. What other reflections do you see?

Photography means "to draw with light." Instead of paints, brush, and canvas, this artist used a camera, film, and sunlight to create his picture, paying careful attention to frame the composition so it would be interesting to look at. What words would you use to describe what is important in this photograph?

CENTRAL SAVINGS

Richard Estes

After all that shopping, this diner is the perfect place to get a bite to eat. Even though the picture looks like a photograph, it's really a painting made to look like a photograph.

And like the photograph you just saw, the city reflections seem to be inside the window, fitting neatly between the counters. Which objects are part of the diner and which are reflections from outside?

As in *Broadway Boogie-Woogie,* this picture uses bright colors, rectangles, and crisscrossing vertical and horizontal lines to make you feel the pulse of the city. In addition to rectangles, circles appear in different parts of the picture. How many can you find?

BOOK STORE
est'd 1894
MENDOZA
BOOK Co.
FORMAL WEA
NESTEA INSTANT

THE BOOKSTORE

Red Grooms

Have you ever seen such a funky bookstore? This life-size "sculptorama" is based on a real New York City bookstore, including browsing customers, a green fire escape, and an outdoor table of sale merchandise. As is often the case in big cities, space is precious, and this store is no exception. Books line the shelves on the upper floor and rest every which way in the crowded windows. In this bookstore you'll have to search carefully for the title of your choice. Can you find a book about Socrates?

The real Mendoza bookstore is a solid structure made of brick, wood, metal, and glass, but its sculptural cousin seems to sway, as if it were a building in a cartoon. To create this feeling of movement, the artist used curving lines instead of the perfectly straight lines you would expect to see on the front of a brick building. Trace your finger over a few of these curving lines. Why do you think the artist painted the bookstore this way?

A SCENE ON THE ICE NEAR A TOWN

Hendrick Avercamp

Trains, cars, buses, horses, boats, and bicycles are just some of the ways people get around cities. Without transportation, cities just wouldn't work. Imagine living in a city where you need ice skates to get around! In this picture of a town in Holland, the ice is in many ways like any other busy city street.

Some of the people skate from this small town to the big city in the distance and back again, taking care of their daily errands and business. How many skaters can you find? Others choose to go by foot. Which type of transportation seems easier? Which looks like more fun?

The artist included many details in the picture that give you a true sense of what a typical day in this town might be like. What kinds of things are happening? There are men, women, children, animals, and even boats on the ice. Certainly boats can't sail on the frozen surface. Why do you think they are there?

CANAL

Maurice Prendergast

In Venice, Italy, people don't need cars, buses, or trains to get around. That's because Venice is built on a group of islands, so the main "roads" are canals. To show the watery nature of Venice, the artist chose to use watercolors. Look at the water in the canal. How does the artist create a feeling of movement?

In Venice people hire special boats called *gondolas,* like the ones you see here, just as in other cities people hail taxis. The gondolier on the right carefully steers his craft to the stairs to let off his passenger. Now he's ready for another fare. Care to climb aboard?

SAINT-LAZARE STATION

Claude Monet

Hey! What are you doing on the tracks? That's exactly where you'd be standing if this painting of a Paris train station came to life. Why do you think the artist chose to show the station from this unique perspective?

This painter was fascinated by the sunlight streaming through the station's iron and glass ceiling, and by the steam coming from the trains' smokestacks. Quick, loose strokes of gray, white, and violet paint rise like pillowy clouds and then begin to disappear. Where does the steam go?

TRANSPORTATION

CHARING CROSS BRIDGE

André Derain

Most people spend their lives on the ground looking up, but in this view of London about a hundred years ago you get to glimpse the city from high above the trees. From here Charing Cross Bridge appears to be a racetrack of zooming miniature motor cars and horse-drawn carriages. What other modes of transportation do you see?

The colors in this picture, as in *Paris through the Window,* are not ones found in nature. Instead of showing the city as it actually looked at the time, the artist created a wonderland of soft colors. Which season of the year do these colors most remind you of?

SIX O'CLOCK, WINTER

John Sloan

It's six o'clock, and in the city that means one thing more than anything else: rush hour. In this painting of a busy train station, you can see crowds of people doing many different things. The commuters at the bottom of the picture move in opposite directions on their way to or from work. What do you think it would feel and sound like to be part of this crowd as a train rumbles onto the platform overhead?

Streetlights glow like tiny yellow moons along the platform, yet the sky is still blue. The painting is called *Six O'Clock, Winter.* Do you think it is six o'clock in the morning or in the evening?

Now that you've seen how some artist see cities, try creating your own unique artwork that captures the excitement and personality of your city or town.

NOTE TO PARENTS AND TEACHERS

As an elementary school teacher I had the opportunity to show my students many examples of great art. I was always amazed by their enthusiastic responses to the colors, shapes, subjects, and fascinating stories of the artists' lives. It wasn't uncommon for us to spend an entire class period looking at and talking about just one work of art. By asking challenging questions, I prompted the children to examine and think very carefully about the art, and then quite naturally they would begin to ask all sorts of interesting questions of their own. These experiences inspired me to write this book and the other volumes in the *How Artists See* series.

How Artists See is designed to teach children about the world by looking at art, and about art by looking at the world through the eyes of great artists. The books encourage children to look critically, answer—and ask—thought-provoking questions, and form an appreciation and understanding of an artist's vision. Each book is devoted to a single subject so that children can see how different artists have approached and treated the same theme, and begin to understand the importance of individual style.

Because I believe that children learn most successfully in an atmosphere of exploration and discovery, I've included questions that encourage them to formulate ideas and responses for themselves. And because people's reactions to art are based on their own personal aesthetic, most of the questions are open-ended and have more than one answer. If you're reading aloud to your children or students, give them ample time to look at each work and form their own opinions; it certainly is not necessary to read the whole book in one sitting. Like a good book or movie, art can be enjoyed over and over again, each time with the possibility of revealing something that wasn't seen before.

You may notice that dates and other historical information are not included in the main text. I purposely omitted this information in order to focus on the art and those aspects of the world it illustrates. For children who want to learn more about the artists whose works appear in the book, short biographies are provided at the end, along with suggestions for further reading and a list of museums where you can see additional works by each artist.

After reading *How Artists See Cities,* children can do a wide variety of related activities to extend and reinforce all that they've learned. In addition to the simple activities I've suggested throughout the main text, they can draw, paint, or construct a cityscape, or, along with a parent, go on a historical tour of their city or town. Since the examples shown here are just a tiny fraction of the great works of art that feature cities as their subject, children can go on a scavenger hunt through museums and the many art books in your local library to find other images of cities.

I hope that you and your children or students will enjoy reading and rereading this book and, by looking at many styles of art, discover how artists share with us their unique ways of seeing and depicting our world.

ARTISTS' BIOGRAPHIES

(in order of appearance)

If you'd like to know more about the artists in this book, here's some information to get you started:

GUSTAVE CAILLEBOTTE (1848–1894), *pp. 4–5*

Many people buy art in the hope that their collection will be worth a lot of money in time. But the French architect and amateur painter Gustave Caillebotte (pronounced *ky-yuh-BOHT*) collected only artwork that appealed to him. As luck would have it, in 1874 he met three young artists who were making paintings with a unusual and altogether original look. The artists were Claude Monet (see *Saint-Lazare Station*), Edgar Degas, and Auguste Renoir. That same year Caillebotte organized the infamous art exhibit that gave these artists the name now known the world over: Impressionists. Until recently Caillebotte's own painting was all but ignored, but a 1994 traveling exhibition introduced his art to thousands of people. His most famous painting, *Paris Street: Rainy Day* beautifully captures the elegance of that city in the nineteenth century. Upon his death Caillebotte left his large collection of Impressionist paintings to the French government; they now hang in the Louvre Museum in Paris.

EDWARD HOPPER (1882–1967), *pp. 6–7*

Empty city streets, light-filled rooms, old houses, and brick buildings are some of the subjects that American artist Edward Hopper painted during his long career. He painted in a realistic way, choosing to show the world as it really looks, at a time when many other artists were moving away from this style. Light was very important to Hopper. Many of his paintings show how light can create moods and feelings. A creature of habit, he worked in his New York City studio for most of the year, except in the summer, when he lived and worked on Cape Cod in Massachusetts. Because of his unique style and familiar subject matter, this painter of American life has become one of the best-known artists of the twentieth century.

ARCHIBALD MOTLEY, JR. (1891–1980), *pp. 8–9*

As a young man growing up in Chicago, Illinois, the African-American artist Archibald Motley, Jr., loved to explore "The Stroll," an area of the city alive with black culture. These early experiences came to mind later, when he painted pictures of dance halls, movie theaters, nightclubs, and jazz musicians. Motley felt that not enough black artists used their own history and culture as subjects, and he devoted his career to celebrating those things in his artwork. He once said, "What a pity so many of our artists go in for pretty landscapes and pictures which have no bearing on our group." With dramatic compositions and bold colors, this very original American artist beautifully expressed the dignity and spirit of a people.

ANDO HIROSHIGE (1797–1858), *pp. 10–11*

In the long history of Japanese art, the master printmaker Ando Hiroshige is considered to be one of the country's greatest artists. During the early part of his career, he was best known for making pictures of beautiful women; later he turned his attention to natural subjects, including birds, flowers, and landscapes. He studied and mastered the style of Japanese painting known as ukioyo-e, which was popular from 1603 to 1867. *Ukiyo-e* means "the floating world," and art from this period depicts happiness and the pleasures of daily life. Hiroshige is most famous for his series "The 53 Stations on the Tōkaidō Highway," a group of prints that include magnificent views of the Japanese countryside. Hiroshige's artwork became popular in France during the late nineteenth century, and it influenced many artists, including the young French painter Claude Monet (see *Saint-Lazare Station*).

ANDREA MANTEGNA (1431–1506), *pp. 12–13*

The Italian Renaissance was a period of great creativity that lasted for nearly two centuries (1400–1600), and one of the greatest artists of this time was the painter Andrea Mantegna. He became a "master" painter at the age of seventeen and received his first major assignment shortly after that. Like many other Renaissance artists, Mantegna was fascinated by the history and culture of ancient Greece and Rome, and would often include images of classical sculpture and architecture, such as arches, columns, and domes, in his paintings. He was one of the first Renaissance artists to use a technique called linear perspective to create the illusion of space, and he planned his compositions with the accuracy of a mathematician. The people in his paintings have the appearance of sculptures, as if he chiseled them from stone. One art critic of the day even referred to his "stony manner." The work of this important artist would become a huge influence on the young Michelangelo, considered by many to be the greatest artist the world has ever known.

MARC CHAGALL (1887–1985), *pp. 14–15*

This popular artist was born into a large, poor Russian family that taught him to love and appreciate the traditions of Jewish life. As a boy he attended art schools in St. Petersburg, a large city in Russia, and then moved to Paris to pursue his career as an artist. He chose the right time to be in Paris, which was the center the art world in the early part of the twentieth century. Chagall quickly became known worldwide as a gifted painter of brightly colored fantasies that combine his memories of childhood with the experiences of living in a vibrant, modern city. This versatile artist also created stained-glass windows, theater sets and costumes, prints, drawings, and ceramics. His works have been widely reproduced, and that has helped make him one of the world's most well-known and beloved artists.

VLADIMIR TATLIN (1885–1953), *pp. 16–17*

Another Russian artist, Vladimir Tatlin, was a painter until he visited the famous artist Pablo Picasso, who urged him to become a sculptor. Picasso also inspired him to use unusual materials to make sculptures, and he began to work with such materials as plaster and broken glass. Tatlin was the first artist to design abstract sculptures. He believed that art should be a useful part of society and that modern sculpture should include movement and be made from industrial materials. He called his approach to art Constructivism. Because of the Russian government's strict regulations during Tatlin's lifetime, many of his designs were never made. Today he is considered one of the most inventive sculptors of the twentieth century.

GEORGIA O'KEEFFE (1887–1986), *p. 18*

When the American painter Georgia O'Keeffe was twelve years old, she told a friend that she would become an artist. She went to art school and later became a teacher. When she was twenty-five years old, she sent some of her water-color paintings to her best friend, who showed them to a gallery owner in New York City. The gallery owner was Alfred Stieglitz, a very famous photographer who would later become her husband. Stieglitz was so impressed with O'Keeffe's pictures that he hung them up in his gallery without even asking her permission! That was the start of her long and amazing career as an artist. Her paintings show ordinary things in unusual ways, such as a single flower that fills up the whole canvas, sun-bleached animal skulls, seashells, and desert hillsides.

PIET MONDRIAN (1872–1944), *p. 19*

When the Dutch painter Piet Mondrian was a young artist, he painted pictures of tree-filled landscapes. Those early works were in a style far different from the one he would become famous for: grids of blue, red, yellow, and white rectangles separated by black lines. Before Mondrian came along, paintings were always pictures of something recognizable: a person, a bowl of fruit, a day at the beach. But Mondrian's paintings were made just from lines, shapes, and colors. These abstract paintings were something entirely new, and the world sat up and took notice. For most of his adult life Mondrian lived in Paris, but then he moved to New York City, where the sounds of jazz and the city's enormous buildings influenced his later paintings (as in *Broadway Boogie-Woogie*). Today, many consider him to be the "father of twentieth-century modern art."

FLORINE STETTHEIMER (1871–1944), *pp. 20–21*

Florine Stettheimer was born into a wealthy New York City family, and New York became her favorite subject to paint during her career as an artist. She attended the Art Students' League, a famous art school that produced many of the twentieth century's most gifted American artists, and then continued her studies in Europe. Her family was very involved in the New York art world, and Florine was friendly with many important artists of the day, including Marcel Duchamp. In 1916 she had her first solo exhibition, which did not get good reviews from the critics; after that she showed her work from her apartment. In addition to being a painter, Stettheimer was a poet and a theatrical designer.

JEAN-EUGÈNE-AUGUSTE ATGET (1857–1927), *pp. 22–23*

"He already had the ambition of creating a collection of everything artistic and picturesque in and about Paris," wrote a friend of the French photographer Eugène Atget (pronounced *aht-ZHAY*) in 1916. To accomplish this goal, Atget used a view camera, which he placed on a tripod, and set about taking pictures of all aspects of Paris. He worked early in the day, to capture the beautiful morning sunlight and to avoid being bothered by onlookers. His favorite subjects were historic buildings, shop windows, parks, fountains, and statues, and he photographed them all with keen attention to detail. Amazingly, Atget never exhibited his photographs or had them published in newspapers or magazines during his lifetime. After he died, the American photographer Berenice Abbott printed his negatives and exhibited his work, introducing Atget's huge body of photography to a new generation of people. Today Atget is considered one of the great photographic artists of the early twentieth century.

RICHARD ESTES (BORN 1936), *pp. 24–25*

Like Atget, who rose early in the morning to photograph the city of Paris, the American painter Richard Estes (pronounced *ES-teez*) "shoots" pictures of the city in the wee hours of the day. But unlike Atget, whose goal was to produce photographs, Estes uses his snapshots to create paintings that have the appearance of photographs. As the leading member of a group of painters called Photorealists, Estes projects a color slide that he has taken on a piece of canvas and then uses an airbrush to paint the picture. His precisely detailed paintings of billboards, shop windows and their reflections, theater marquees, sidewalks, and storefronts depict parts of the city that aren't considered beautiful—just everyday sights that most people hardly stop to notice. In this way his subject matter is similar to that of an earlier American painter, Edward Hopper, who also captured snapshotlike scenes of American city life (see *Early Sunday Morning*).

RED GROOMS (BORN 1937), *pp. 26–27*

This American artist began to draw as a young boy, and at age ten his mother enrolled him in art classes at the local museum. In the eighth grade his model of a circus won first prize in a hobby fair, and he had his first art exhibit while he was still in high school. From then on, Red Grooms was in and out of art schools, never finding one that could hold his interest. Instead of finishing art school, he moved to New York City, where he began making all kinds of art, including paintings, sculptures, and his famous "constructions," whole environments that look like miniature theater sets. Some of his favorite subjects are life in New York City and humorous portraits of family and friends.

HENDRICK AVERCAMP (1585–1634), *pp. 28–29*

Known during his lifetime as "the mute of Kampen," the Dutch painter Hendrick Avercamp (pronounced *AH-ver-kahmp*), was quite a popular artist in his day. Best known for detailed winter scenes that show people working and playing, he was one of the first artists in Holland to paint landscapes in a realistic style. He would often make small drawings on paper and then tint them with watercolors, which was a popular and collectible art form in seventeenth-century Holland, and his paintings and drawings were in demand by private art collectors. Today one of the best collections of his small-scale artworks is held at Windsor Castle, England's historic royal residence.

MAURICE PRENDERGAST (1859–1924), *pp. 30–31*

Maurice Prendergast was born in Canada, but lived and worked in America. In the early twentieth century he was part of a group of artists known as The Eight. These eight painters believed that artists should paint exactly what they choose to, instead of following the popular styles of the day. They also were known as the

Ashcan School, because many of their paintings captured the grimy, dark side of city life. Prendergast stood out from the group because his paintings were full of bright patches of color that seemed to glow and move, much like the French Impressionists, whose work he admired (look back at *Saint-Lazare Station*). Today, Maurice Prendergast is known as an American Impressionist.

CLAUDE MONET (1840–1926), *p. 32*

After a painting called *Impression: Sunrise* by Claude Monet (pronounced *mo-NAY*) was shown in an art exhibit, he and the other artists in the show became known as Impressionists. This group of French artists made pictures that show how sunlight appears at different times of day, during different seasons of the year, and on many different kinds of objects and surfaces, such as morning light on a river or afternoon light on a stone building. Monet liked to work outdoors, and he painted with small brush strokes of pure color that came right out of the tube. He didn't mix his colors (which was the custom of the day), but let the colors blend together in the viewer's eye. Some of his most famous paintings are of waterlilies, haystacks, and the front of a great cathedral in the French town of Rouen. Monet is known as the founder of Impressionism, the style that began what is now known as modern art.

ANDRÉ DERAIN (1880–1954), *p. 33*

1899 was a good year for the French artist André Derain; that was the year he met Henri Matisse. Matisse, who would become one of the most important artists of the twentieth century, encouraged Derain to take painting seriously. Along with Matisse and other young artists, he became a member of the Fauves (which in French means "wild beasts"). They got their name because they used pure, bold colors and often painted their subjects in colors that don't occur in nature, such as a green sky or a person with purple skin. For most of his career Derain painted in whatever style was in fashion, except for a short period when he developed the style that he is now famous for: landscapes of vivid colors and patchworklike brush strokes.

JOHN SLOAN (1871–1951), *pp. 34–35*

John Sloan began his career as an illustrator and cartoonist for newspapers and magazines in Philadelphia. After moving to New York City in 1904, he continued this line of work, but began painting as often as possible. For inspiration he would walk throughout the city and write down his observations in a journal. He was especially drawn to the poor neighborhoods, and the underprivileged people who lived in them became the main subjects of his work. He once said that as a painter he was "making pictures from life," and he depicted the working class with dignity. Like Maurice Prendergast he was a member of The Eight, a group that became known for their realistic paintings of New York in the early twentieth century. His dramatic pictures influenced the work of another great painter of American city life, Edward Hopper (see *Early Sunday Morning*).

SUGGESTIONS FOR FURTHER READING

The following children's titles are excellent sources for learning more about the artists presented in this book.

FOR EARLY READERS (AGES 4–7)

Bjork, Christina. *Linnea in Monet's Garden.* New York: R&S Books, 1987.
A little girl named Linnea visits Claude Monet's garden in the French town of Giverny and learns about his life and art along the way. This title is also available on videotape.

Hoban, Tana. *Shadows and Reflections.* New York: Greenwillow Books, 1990.
This text-free picture book contains many visually interesting still photographs of a variety of reflections and shadows.

Sellier, Marie. *Chagall from A to Z.* Translated from the French by Claudia Zoe Bedrick. New York: Peter Bedrick Books, 1996.
In this charming and beautifully illustrated book, the letters of the alphabet introduce elements of the Russian painter's long life and career.

Venezia, Mike. *Edward Hopper.* Getting to Know the World's Greatest Artists series. Chicago: Children's Press, 1990.
This easy-to-read biography combines color reproductions and humorous illustrations to capture the personality and talent of the famous twentieth-century American artist.

FOR INTERMEDIATE READERS (AGES 8–10)

Koja, Stephen, and Katja Miksovsky. *Claude Monet: The Magician of Colour.* Adventure in Art series. Munich: Prestel-Verlag, 1997.
This book takes readers on a journey through the life of the French Impressionist painter, beginning with his early years as an artist. Readers will learn about professional and personal aspects of the artist's life, and be introduced to many of his most famous works.

Mason, Anthony. *Monet: An Introduction to the Artist's Life and Work.* Famous Artists series. Hauppauge, New York: Barron's, 1995.
This wonderful book provides a wealth of information about the French Impressionist painter.

Zubrowski, Bernie, and Roy Doty (illustrator). *Shadow Play: Making Pictures with Light and Lenses.* A Boston Children's Museum Activity Book. New York: William Morrow, 1995.
This activity book teaches the basic scientific concepts of light and reflection, and explains how lenses work. The playful illustrations create appealing and informative visual aids that help make the fun activities easy to understand.

FOR ADVANCED READERS (AGES 11+)

Czech, Kenneth P. *Snapshot: America Discovers the Camera.* Minneapolis: Lerner Publications Company, 1997.
This book chronicles the fascinating history of photography, from its birth in nineteenth-century France to its popularity today.

Hilton, Jonathan, and Barrie Watts, eds. *Photography: A First Guide.* Highland Park, N.J.: Mill Brook Press, 1995.
A how-to guide for young photographers. This book offers tips on taking good pictures, composing shots, and developing and printing film.

Mühlberger, Richard. *What Makes a Monet a Monet.* New York: The Metropolitan Museum of Art and Viking, 1994.
The work of the French painter is explored in a way that teaches children to recognize his unique style.

Turner, Robyn Montana. *Georgia O'Keeffe.* Portraits of Women Artists for Children series. Boston: Little, Brown and Company, 1991.
The fascinating story of O'Keeffe's life is told and illustrated with many of her most well-known paintings.

WHERE TO SEE THE ARTISTS' WORK

EUGÈNE ATGET

- Ackland Museum, The University of North Carolina at Chapel Hill
- The Art Institute of Chicago
- George Eastman House, Rochester, New York
- Museum of Modern Art, New York
- Philadelphia Museum of Art

HENDRICK AVERCAMP

- National Gallery, London
- Rijksmuseum, Amsterdam
- Windsor Castle, England

GUSTAVE CAILLEBOTTE

- The Art Institute of Chicago
- Kimbell Art Museum, Fort Worth, Texas
- Milwaukee Art Center
- Minneapolis Institute of Arts
- Musée d'Orsay, Paris
- Musée du Petit Palais, Geneva
- Museum of Fine Arts, Boston
- Museum of Fine Arts, Houston
- National Gallery of Art, Washington, D.C.
- Virginia Museum of Fine Arts, Richmond
- http://watt.emf.net/wm/paint/auth/caillebotte

MARC CHAGALL

- The Art Institute of Chicago
- Solomon R. Guggenheim Museum, New York
- Haggerty Museum of Art, Marquette University, Milwaukee, Wisconsin
- McNay Art Museum, San Antonio, Texas
- Masur Museum of Art, Monroe, Louisiana
- Metropolitan Opera House, Lincoln Center, New York
- Museum of Modern Art, New York
- Stedelijk Museum, Amsterdam
- The Union Church, Pocantico Hills, New York

ANDRÉ DERAIN

- Musée d'Art Moderne de la Ville de Paris
- Musée d'Orsay, Paris
- Musée National d'Art Moderne, Centre Georges Pompidou, Paris
- Museum of Fine Arts, Houston
- Museum of Modern Art, New York
- National Gallery of Canada, Ottawa
- Philadelphia Museum of Art
- Statens Museum for Kunst, Copenhagen

RICHARD ESTES

- The Art Institute of Chicago
- Des Moines Art Center
- High Museum of Art, Atlanta
- Solomon R. Guggenheim Museum, New York
- Museum of Modern Art, New York
- Museum Moderner Kunst, Vienna
- National Museum of American Art, Smithsonian Institution, Washington, D.C.
- Nelson-Atkins Museum of Art, Kansas City, Missouri
- San Antonio Museum Association, San Antonio, Texas
- Toledo Museum of Art, Toledo, Ohio
- Whitney Museum of American Art, New York

RED GROOMS

- Art Museum of Southeast Texas, Beaumont
- Brooklyn Museum, New York
- Cleveland Center for Contemporary Art
- Hudson River Museum of Westchester, Yonkers, New York
- Pennsylvania Academy of the Fine Arts, Philadelphia
- Sawhill Gallery, James Madison University, Harrisonburg, Virginia

ANDO HIROSHIGE

- The Art Institute of Chicago
- British Museum, London
- Freer Gallery of Art, Smithsonian Institution, Washington, D.C.
- Los Angeles County Museum of Art
- The Metropolitan Museum of Art, New York
- Musée Guimet, Paris
- Museum of Fine Arts, Boston
- The Abby Aldrich Rockefeller Collection of Japanese Prints, Museum of Art, Rhode Island School of Design, Providence
- Tokyo Imperial House Museum
- Victoria and Albert Museum, London
- Wight Art Gallery Complex, University of Southern California, Los Angeles

EDWARD HOPPER

- Addison Gallery of American Art, Phillips Academy, Andover, Massachusetts
- Delaware Art Museum, Wilmington
- Hopper House/Edward Hopper Preservation Foundation, Nyack, New York
- The Huntington Library Art Collections and Botanical Gardens, San Marino, California
- Montclair Art Museum, New Jersey
- Portland Museum of Art, Portland, Maine
- University of Arizona Museum of Fine Art, Tucson
- Whitney Museum of American Art, New York
- Yale University Art Gallery, New Haven, Connecticut

ANDREA MANTEGNA

- Brera Gallery, Milan
- Camera degli Sposi, Palazzo Ducale, Mantua
- Louvre Museum, Paris
- National Gallery, London
- Ovetari Chapel, Eremitani Church, Padua
- Church of San Zeno, Verona
- Uffizi Gallery, Florence

PIET MONDRIAN

- The Art Institute of Chicago
- Carnegie Museum of Art, Pittsburgh
- Dallas Museum of Art
- Gemeente Museum, The Hague, The Netherlands
- Guggenheim Museum Soho, New York
- The Solomon R. Guggenheim Museum, New York
- Kröller-Müller Museum, Otterlo, The Netherlands
- Minneapolis Institute of Arts
- Munson-Williams-Proctor Institute Museum, Utica, New York
- Museum of Modern Art, New York
- National Gallery of Art, Washington, D.C.
- Philadelphia Museum of Art
- The Phillips Collection, Washington, D.C.
- Toledo Museum of Art, Toledo, Ohio
- Wadsworth Atheneum, Hartford, Connecticut

CLAUDE MONET

- Dallas Museum of Art
- Dixon Gallery and Gardens, Memphis
- High Museum of Art, Atlanta
- The Metropolitan Museum of Art, New York
- Musée d'Orsay, Paris

- Museum of Fine Arts, Boston
- Museum of Fine Arts, St. Petersburg, Florida
- Museum of Modern Art, New York
- North Carolina Museum of Art, Raleigh
- Philadelphia Museum of Art
- Shelburne Museum, Vermont
- Tate Gallery, London
- University of Rochester Memorial Art Gallery, New York

ARCHIBALD MOTLEY, JR.

- Ackland Art Museum, The University of North Carolina at Chapel Hill
- The Art Institute of Chicago
- Chicago Historical Society
- Illinois Art Gallery, Chicago
- National Museum of American Art, Smithsonian Institution, Washington, D.C.
- Schomburg Center for Research in Black Culture, The New York Public Library
- Western Illinois University Art Gallery and Museum, Macomb

GEORGIA O'KEEFFE

- Albuquerque Museum of Art, History, and Science, New Mexico
- Amon Carter Museum, Fort Worth
- Birmingham Museum of Art, Alabama
- Brooklyn Museum of Art, New York
- National Museum of Women in the Arts, Washington, D.C
- New Jersey State Museum, Trenton
- The Phillips Collection, Washington, D.C.
- Phoenix Art Museum
- Reynolda House Museum of American Art, Winston-Salem, North Carolina
- Carl Van Vechten Gallery of Fine Arts, Fisk University, Nashville

MAURICE PRENDERGAST

- Cape Ann Historical Association, Gloucester, Massachusetts
- William A. Farnsworth Library and Art Museum, Rockland, Maine
- Maier Museum of Art, Randolph Macon Women's College, Lynchburg, Virginia
- Munson-Williams-Proctor Institute Museum, Utica, New York
- Museum of Fine Arts, Boston
- Reynolda House Museum of American Art, Winston-Salem, North Carolina
- Terra Museum of American Art, Chicago

JOHN SLOAN

- Brooklyn Museum, New York
- Butler Institute of American Art, Youngstown, Ohio
- Delaware Art Museum, Wilmington
- Charles H. MacNider Museum, Mason City, Iowa
- The Phillips Collection, Washington, D.C.
- Southern Alleghenies Museum of Art, Loretto, Pennsylvania
- Wadsworth Atheneum, Hartford, Connecticut

FLORINE STETTHEIMER

- The Art Institute of Chicago
- Beinecke Rare Book and Manuscript Library, Yale College of American Literature, New Haven, Connecticut
- Cleveland Museum of Art
- Detroit Institute of Art
- The Metropolitan Museum of Art, New York
- Museum of Fine Arts, Boston
- Museum of Modern Art, New York
- Nelson-Atkins Museum of Art, Kansas City
- Philadelphia Museum of Art
- Whitney Museum of American Art, New York

VLADIMIR TATLIN

- Musée National d'Art Moderne, Centre Georges Pompidou, Paris

CREDITS *(listed in order of appearance)*

Gustave Caillebotte (1848–1894). *Paris Street; Rainy Day*, 1876–77. Oil on canvas, 83½ × 108¾ in. (212.2 × 276.2 cm). The Art Institute of Chicago; Charles H. and Mary F. S. Worcester Collection (1964.336). Photograph © 1997 The Art Institute of Chicago. Edward Hopper (1882–1967). *Early Sunday Morning*, 1930. Oil on canvas, 35 × 60 in. (88.9 × 152.4 cm). Collection of Whitney Museum of American Art, New York; Purchase, with funds from Gertrude Vanderbilt Whitney (31.426). Photograph © 1998 Whitney Museum of American Art, New York. Archibald Motley, Jr. (1891–1980). *The Jockey Club*, 1929. Oil on canvas, 25¾ × 32 in. (65.4 × 81.2 cm). Art and Artifacts Division, Schomburg Center for Research in Black Culture, The New York Public Library, Astor, Lenox and Tilden Foundations. Photograph © Manu Sassoonian. Ando Hiroshige (1797–1858). *Moonlit Street Scene in Edo*, 1856. Color woodblock print, 14 × 9¾ in. (35.6 × 24.9 cm). Victoria and Albert Museum, London. Photograph © Victoria and Albert Museum, London/Art Resource, New York. Andrea Mantegna (1431–1506). *L'Incontro Marchese Ludovico Gonzaga Meeting Son, Cardinal Francesco G.*, detail, 1464–74. Fresco. Camera degli Sposi, Palazzo Ducale, Mantua, Italy. Photograph © Scala/Art Resource, New York. Marc Chagall (1887–1985). *Paris Through the Window*, 1913. Oil on canvas, 53½ × 55¾ in. (135.8 × 141.4 cm). Solomon R. Guggenheim Museum, New York; Gift, Solomon R. Guggenheim, 1937. Photograph by David Heald © The Solomon R. Guggenheim Foundation, New York (FN 37.438). © 1998 Artists Rights Society (ARS), New York/ADAGP, Paris. Vladimir Tatlin (1885–1953). *Monument to the Third International*, 1919. Wood, iron, and glass, height 13 ft. 9 in. (4.2 m). Musée National d'Art Moderne, Centre Georges Pompidou, Paris. Photograph © Photothèque des collections du MNAM-CCI. © Estate of Vladimir Tatlin/Licensed by VAGA, New York. Georgia O'Keeffe (1887–1986). *Radiator Building, Night, New York*, 1927. Oil on canvas, 48 × 30. (122 × 76.2 cm). Collection of Fisk University, Nashville, Tennessee. © 1998 The Georgia O'Keeffe Foundation/Artists Rights Society (ARS), New York. Piet Mondrian (1872-1944). *Broadway Boogie-Woogie*, 1942–43. Oil on canvas, 50 × 50 in. (127 × 127 cm). The Museum of Modern Art, New York; Given anonymously. Photograph © 1998 The Museum of Modern Art, New York. © 1998 Mondrian/Holtzman Trust-Artists Rights Society (ARS), New York. Florine Stettheimer (1871–1944). *Spring Sale at Bendel's*, 1921. Oil on canvas, 50 × 40 in. (127 × 101.6 cm). Philadelphia Museum of Art; Given by Miss Ettie Stettheimer. Jean-Eugène-Auguste Atget (1857-1927). *Magasin, avenue des Gobelins*, 1925. Albumen-silver print, 9⅜ × 7 in. (24 × 18 cm). The Museum of Modern Art, New York; Abbott-Levy Collection; Partial gift of Shirley C. Burden. Copy print © 1998 The Museum of Modern Art, New York. Richard Estes (b. 1936). *Central Savings*, 1975. Oil on canvas, 36 × 48 in. (91.4 × 121.9 cm). Nelson-Atkins Museum of Art, Kansas City, Missouri. © Richard Estes; Courtesy, Marlborough Gallery, New York. Red Grooms (b. 1937). *The Bookstore*, 1978–79. Sculpto-pictorama: mixed media, 25 × 20 × 11 ft. (7.6 × 6.1 × 3.4 m). The Hudson River Museum of Westchester, Yonkers, New York; Funding for *The Bookstore* was made possible by a grant from the National Endowment for the Arts, matched by contributions from the William Randolph Hearst Foundation, Sarah I. Schieffelin Residuary Trust, Wells, Rich, Green, Inc., Gestetner Corporation, and IBM Corporation. © 1998 Red Grooms/Artists Rights Society (ARS), New York. Hendrick Avercamp (1585–634). *A Scene on the Ice Near a Town*, c. 1615. Oil on oak, 22¾ × 35⅜ in. (58 × 89.8 cm). The National Gallery, London. Maurice Prendergast (1859–1924). *Canal*, 1912. Watercolor and graphite on paper, 15½ × 22 in. (39.4 × 55.9 cm). Munson-Williams-Proctor Institute Museum of Art, Utica, New York; Edward W. Root Bequest (57.213). Claude Monet (1840–1926). *Saint-Lazare Station*, 1877. Oil on canvas, 29½ × 40⅞ in. (75 × 104 cm). Musée d'Orsay, Paris. Photograph © Hubert Josse/Abbeville Press, New York. André Derain (1880–1954). *Charing Cross Bridge*, c. 1906. Oil on canvas, 31⅞ × 39⅜ in. (81 × 100 cm). Musée d'Orsay, Paris. Photograph © Hubert Josse/Abbeville Press, New York. © 1998 Artists Rights Society (ARS), New York/ADAGP, Paris. John Sloan (1871–1951). *Six O'Clock, Winter*, 1912. Oil on canvas, 26 × 32 in. (66 × 81.2 cm). The Phillips Collection, Washington, D.C.